Since the mid-1980s in-line skating has become very popular. It is now one of the fastest-growing sports in the world.

So what is it all about, and how can you be a part of it?

In-line skating is about having fun. There are many different types of skating to enjoy. You can skate to get fit – it's better for you than running or cycling.

Try picking up a stick and playing in-line hockey with a team. Or join a speed skating club and get into racing.

This book is about aggressive skating. Aggressive skating is about doing tricks and stunts, in skateparks or on the streets. You need to be brave, maybe a little crazy. That's what makes it one of the most exciting sports around.

aggressive skating

When skating became popular, some riders tried jumping over objects in the street. The riders started to use the skate parks built for skateboarders and rollerskaters. This type of skating is aggressive skating.

There are now two main types of aggressive skating – street and halfpipe.

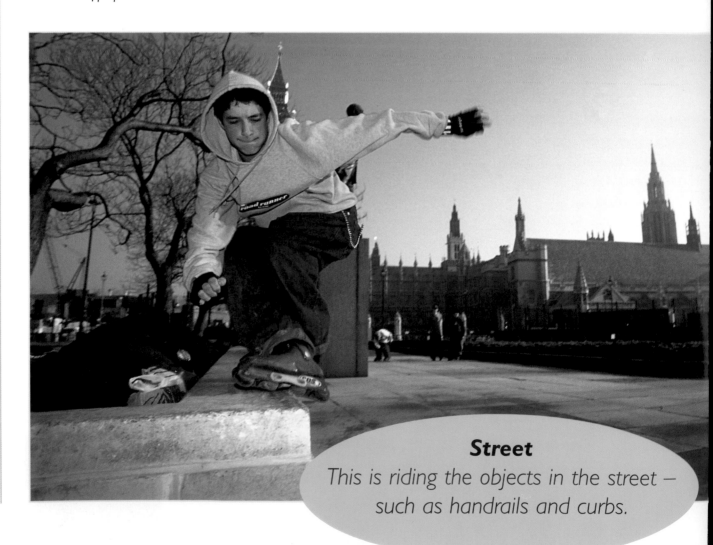

Street
This is riding the objects in the street – such as handrails and curbs.

Halfpipe
Halfpipes are big 'U' shaped ramps. Skaters ride up the sides of the ramp, then jump out and do tricks.

5

skates

Aggressive skates have to be tough and comfortable. They have a low frame and small wheels. This keeps you more stable when you land from a height. There's more room between the centre wheels for grinding (see pages 20-21).

These skates often come with grind plates which stop your skates from wearing down. They help you lock onto grinds.

All aggressive skates have laces and a buckle around the top to support your feet. Some have a strap around the heel.

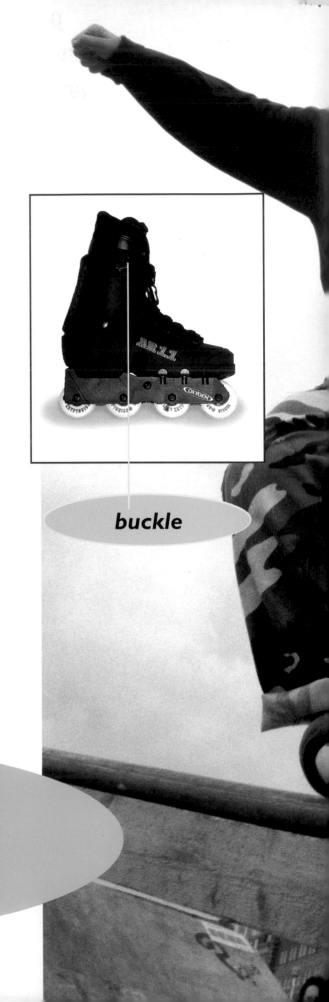

buckle

When buying any skates, make sure they fit you. If they don't, you'll never enjoy skating in them.

wheel

grind plate

frame

laces

safety

Even the best skaters fall over. Skating can be dangerous so make sure you're wearing all the right safety gear. You'll need big knee and elbow pads, wrist guards and a helmet. You can buy padded shorts.

Once you have your pads, you should learn how to fall properly. When you feel yourself about to fall, allow yourself to drop onto your knee pads. Let them take most of the fall.

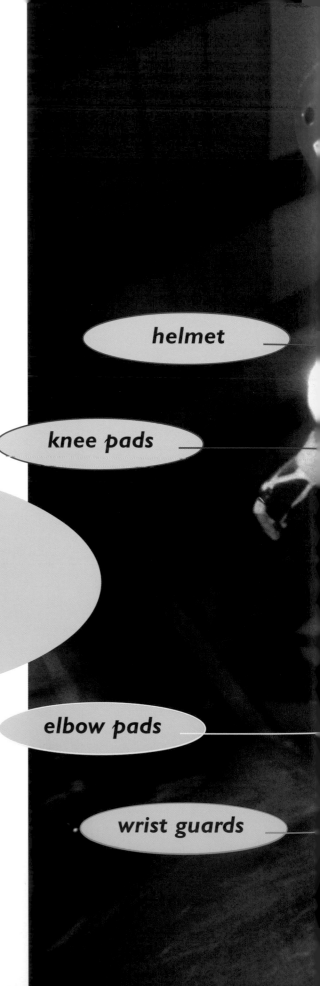

helmet

knee pads

elbow pads

wrist guards

getting started

Before you try anything aggressive, you must learn the basic skills. Without them you will never be a good skater. You must be comfortable skating on flat ground, and up and down hills.

Stopping
Two good ways to stop are –

The t-stop
This is where you drag one skate sideways behind you.

The cess slide
This is where you slide sideways on both skates.

Skating backwards
Skating backwards is often called fakie. You will need to know how to skate fakie to do a lot of the tricks. You need to be happy landing backwards from jumps.

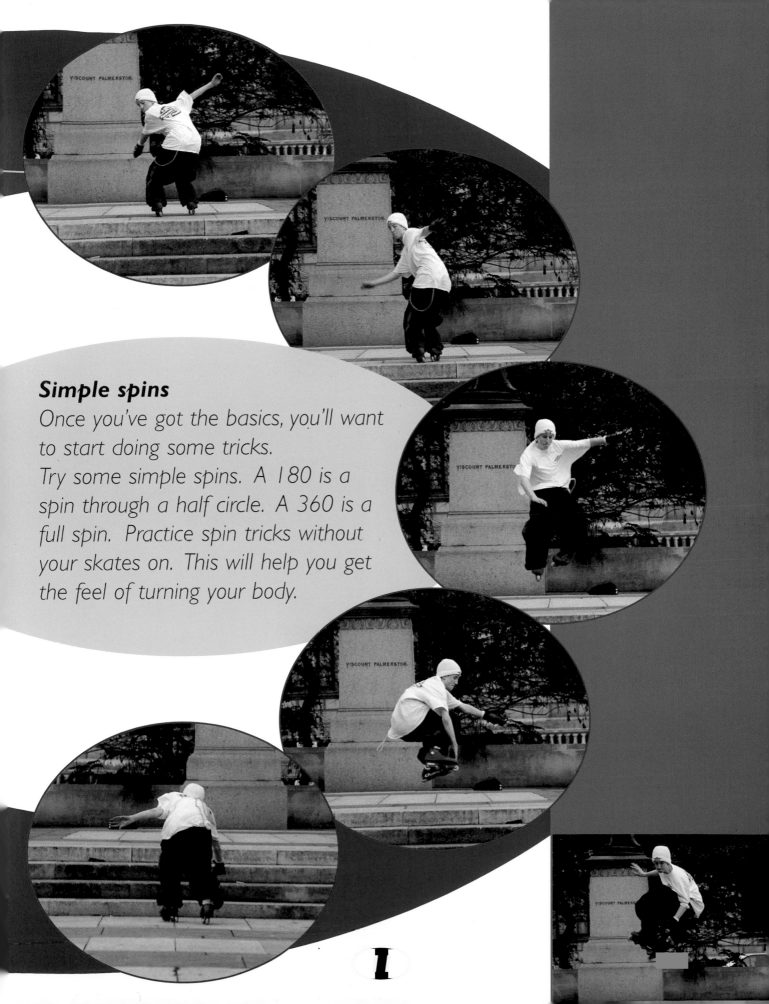

Simple spins

Once you've got the basics, you'll want to start doing some tricks. Try some simple spins. A 180 is a spin through a half circle. A 360 is a full spin. Practice spin tricks without your skates on. This will help you get the feel of turning your body.

the rules of skating

Skate parks

There are a few rules for skating at a skate park –

1 You must wear a helmet.

2 A parent will need to sign a special form. This means that if you fall and hurt yourself, it is not the fault of the park owners.

3 Always keep your eyes and ears open. Skate parks can get very busy with people skating in all directions. Be careful.

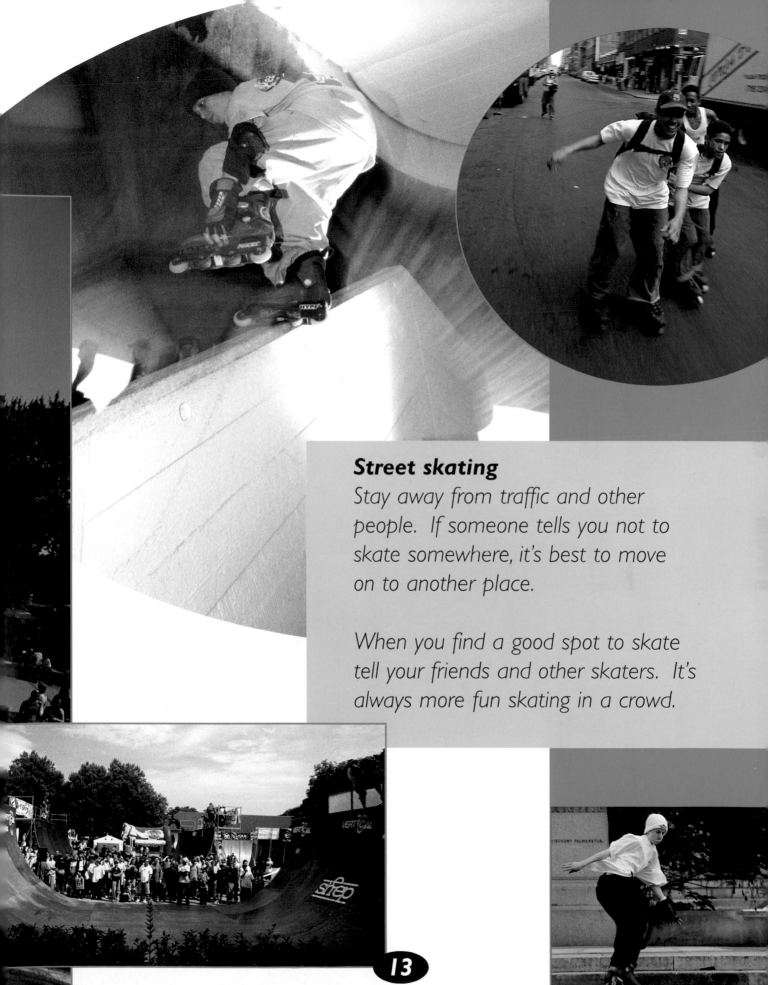

Street skating

Stay away from traffic and other people. If someone tells you not to skate somewhere, it's best to move on to another place.

When you find a good spot to skate tell your friends and other skaters. It's always more fun skating in a crowd.

getting air

Nothing beats the thrill of flying through the air. Jumping and landing are easy if you remember a few things.

- *You only need to jump up — your speed should carry you over or off an object.*
- *Bending your knees will help you land more smoothly.*
- *Start with small objects. Move onto bigger objects when you feel ready.*

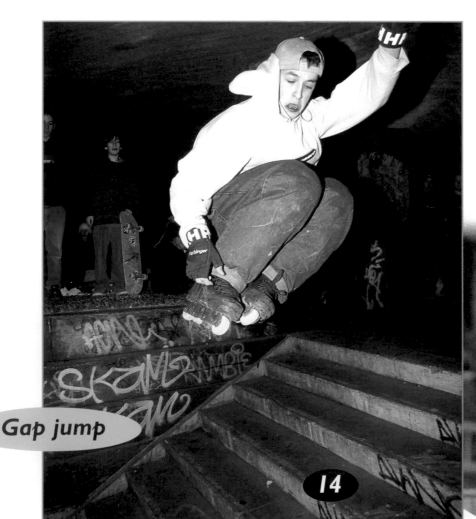

Gap jump

Safety grab

Mute air

Curved ramps

It takes time to get used to skating any curved ramp. To begin with, you should skate up to the top and just let yourself roll back down.

When you have a feel for the curve you can try jumping it. Pretend you're skating through the ramp rather than trying to jump over it. Your speed will carry you over.

When you can do this, it's time to give it some style. Try lifting your knees to your chest and grabbing your feet.

15

halfpipes

The first time you ride a halfpipe, never drop straight into the ramp. Instead, start at the bottom and work your way up.

1. Skate towards one side of the ramp.

2. When you reach the top, turn your body.

3. Look back down the ramp.

4. Push your body into the curve as you come back down.

You should also learn to ride fakie down the ramp. Instead of turning at the top, scissor your feet and look back the way you came.

Dropping in

1 Place one foot on the edge of the ramp.

2 Lean forwards and bend your knees.

3 As you drop into the ramp look towards the bottom of it.

4 Once you're in the ramp, look across it to where you are going.

big ramps
big air

Big ramps mean big thrills. The best riders can jump over three metres into the air from the biggest ramps. Once in the air, they make amazing shapes with their bodies.

Mute air

Air

Mute air

Stale japan

19

grinding

Grinding is just that – riding on an object by grinding along it. Grinding can be done on almost anything from curbs and walls to ramps and rails. You can grind on the gap between your middle wheels, or on the boot itself.

Start with a small object like a curb or a low, flat rail. Jump on the object and try to stay still. This will get you used to jumping to the right foot position. Next time, skate up alongside the object and jump on in the same way. Now try to slide along.

The first two grinds you should learn are the frontside and soul slide.

Frontside

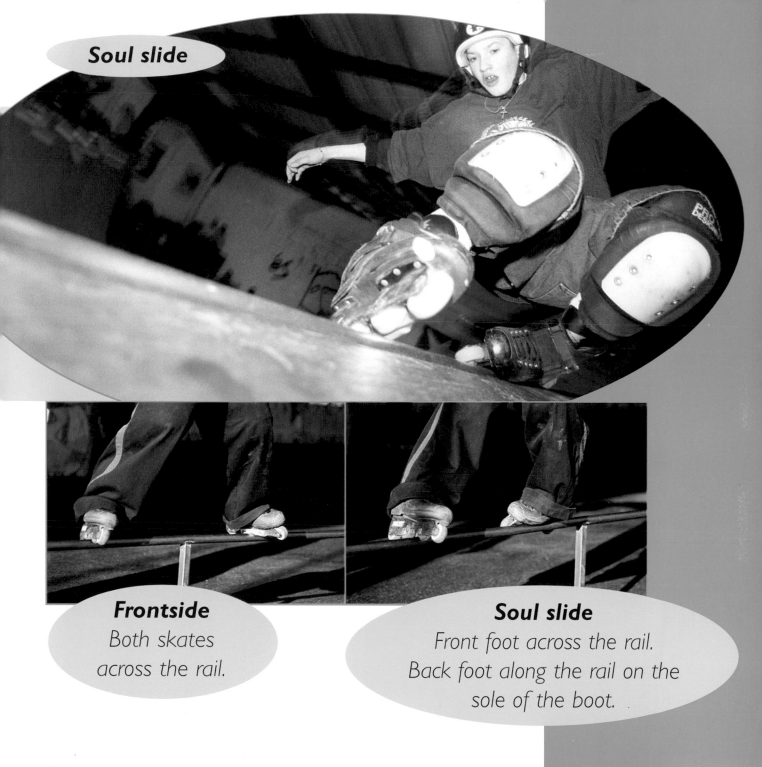

Soul slide

Frontside
Both skates
across the rail.

Soul slide
Front foot across the rail.
Back foot along the rail on the
sole of the boot.

hard grinds

Once you can do the frontside and soul slide, you'll want to try something more difficult and more thrilling.

Mizous, acid souls, and acid mizous are some of the harder grinds.

Once you can do those, try spicing up your grinds with these moves —

Switch tricks *These are where you change the grind while on the rail.*

Revert *This means coming off the grind backwards.*

Rewind *This is where you spin out of the grind.*

Mizou

Acid soul

Acid mizou

Switch trick

give it some style

The tricks here are some of the most stylish. You may need to loosen the top buckles of your skates. This will help your feet to move more easily.

Royale

For royales and backslides you may need to file out a groove on the frame of your back boot. This will help you to lock onto the grind.

Unity

Backslide

Royale

Backslide

Unity

25

more grinds

The more moves you know, the more fun you can have.
Try out your grinds on different types of objects.

Makio

Fishbrain

Makio

Topside acid

tricks plus

Misty flip

28

Hip transfer

Hand plant

Parallel

Once you're doing the tricks on this page, you are ready to enter competitions. Competitions are great places to meet other skaters and see what they can do. Who knows, if you do well, it could soon be you on the pages of magazines and books.

just do it

We can't show you every trick, but this book should give you some idea of what you can do. Look at these pictures and watch the skate videos from your local skate shop. Then go out there, skate safely and skate for fun.

One last tip. If it feels right, it is right. If it feels good, it is good. And if you get that, you'll have fun.

360

Fahrvergnügen

Kind grind

540

31

extra stuff

Disclaimer

Text: Ben Roberts
All photos kindly donated by Ben Roberts
(Ben is an International In-line Skating
Association Level 2 qualified instructor)

Series editor: Matthew Parselle
Art director: Robert Walster
Designer: Andy Stagg
Reading consultant: Frances James

This edition published in 2000 by Franklin Watts
© Franklin Watts 1997
Franklin Watts
96 Leonard Street
London EC2A 4RH
A CIP catalogue for
this book is available
from the British Library

Franklin Watts Australia
14 Mars Road
Lane Cove NSW 2066
ISBN 0 7496 2832 4 (Hb)
       0 7496 3612 2 (Pb)
Dewey classification 796.91
Printed in Dubai

Useful contacts

Maverik Productions
(skate videos)
Tel: 01273 325260

Bondi Boards & Blades
(Australia)
Tel: 02 9365 6555

Index

aggressive skating 4-5
basic skills 10-11
buckles 6
cess slide 10
competitions 29
dropping in 17
fakie 10, 16
falling 8
getting air 14-15,
    18-19
grind plates 6, 7
grinding 6, 20-21
grinds
    acid mizou 22
    acid soul 22
    backslide 24, 25
    fahrvergnügen 31
    fishbrain 27
    frontside 20, 21
    kind grind 31

makio 26, 27
mizou 22
revert 22
rewind 22
royale 24, 25
soul slide 20, 21
switch tricks 22, 23
topside 26
topside acid 27
unity 24, 25
see also tricks
halfpipe 5, 16-17
helmet 8, 12
jumping 14, 15, 20
laces 6, 7
landing 14
pads 8, 9
ramps 5, 15, 16,
    18-19
rules of skating 12

safety 8-9
skate parks 4, 12
    rules in 12
skates 6-7
skating backwards 10
spins 11, 30, 31
stopping 10
street skating 4, 13
t-stop 10
tricks 28-29
    air 19
    gap jump 14
    hand plant 29
    hip transfer 29
    misty flip 28
    parallel 29
    safety grab 15
    stale japan 19
    see also grinds, spins
wheels 6, 7

Thanks to all the skaters who have helped with this book.
Thanks to all at Rehab, Puberty and Road Runner.